PICTURE-PUZZLE RIDDLE BOOK

written and illustrated by

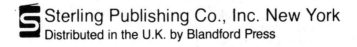

JOYCE BEHR

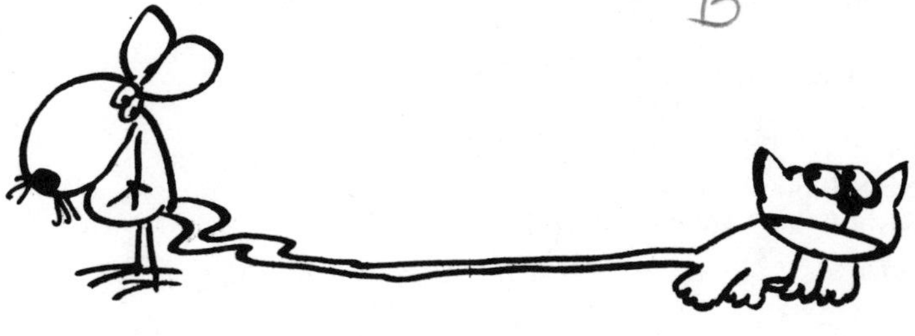

Sterling Publishing Co., Inc. New York
Distributed in the U.K. by Blandford Press

Other Books Illustrated by Joyce Behr
Bananas Don't Grow on Trees
Biggest Riddle Book in the World
Calculator Puzzles, Tricks & Games
Daffy Definitions
Doctor Knock-Knock's Official
  Knock-Knock Dictionary
Funny Insults & Snappy Put-Downs
Gigantic Joke Book
Monster Madness
Polar Bears Like It Hot
Ridiculous Nicholas Pet Riddles
Ridiculous Nicholas Riddle Book
Silly Songbook
Silly Verse (and Even Worse)

Library of Congress Cataloging in Publication Data

Behr, Joyce
  Picture puzzle riddle book.

  Includes index.
  Summary: Hundreds of riddles with answers in rebus form.
  1. Riddles, Juvenile. 2. Rebuses. [1. Riddles. 2. Rebuses] I. Title.
PN6371.5.B38 1983 818'.5402 83-9160
ISBN 0-8069-4676-8
ISBN 0-8069-4677-6 (lib. bdg.)

Two Park Avenue, New York, N.Y. 10016
Distributed in Australia by Oak Tree Press Co., Ltd.
P.O. Box K514 Haymarket, Sydney 2000, N.S.W.
Distributed in the United Kingdom by Blandford Press
Link House, West Street, Poole, Dorset BH15 ILL, England
Distributed in Canada by Oak Tree Press Ltd.
℅ Canadian Manda Group, P.O. Box 920, Station U
Toronto, Ontario, Canada M8Z 5P9
Manufactured in the United States of America

CONTENTS

For Behrs, Behrs,
everywheres!

HOW TO USE THIS BOOK

Before people invented words, they made pictures:

Cave men and women used pictures to communicate ideas:

Later, the Egyptians used picture-symbols called hieroglyphics:

A rebus is a kind of picture-writing using both

WORDS &

Letters can be added or subtracted with a plus (+) or minus (–) sign. For example:

– G
+ S

(glove)

(love)

(gloves)

This set of pictures is called a rebus.

In this book every riddle is in words—every answer is a rebus—

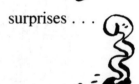

except for one

or two

surprises . . .

You can sound out a rebus—sometimes. Sometimes you need to spell it out. If you can't figure out the words, you can find the correct answers printed upside down below each puzzle, so you won't have to

for them.

We think this  will give you some fun riddles and sharpen your wits at the same time.

These picture puzzles are not kid stuff, and doing them in your head doesn't always work. We tried it and had to sneak a  to figure them out.

So get on your 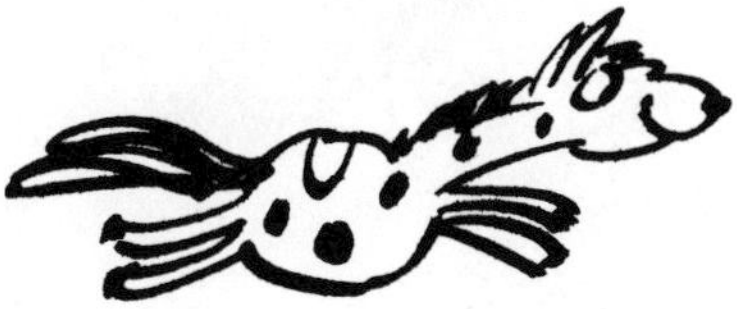, and

STOP
?

!!

QUICKIES

1.

What did the rope say to the squirrel?

2
U!

NUTS (KNOTS) TO YOU!

What color is the north wind?

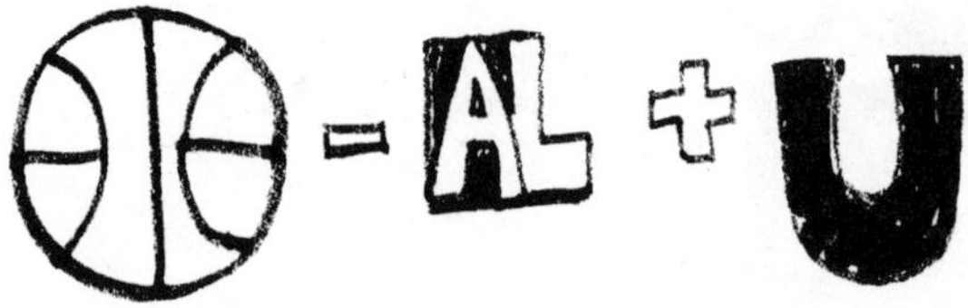
AL
U

BLUE

What kind of bow can be neither tied nor untied?

A

A RAINBOW

What flowers do you wear on your face?

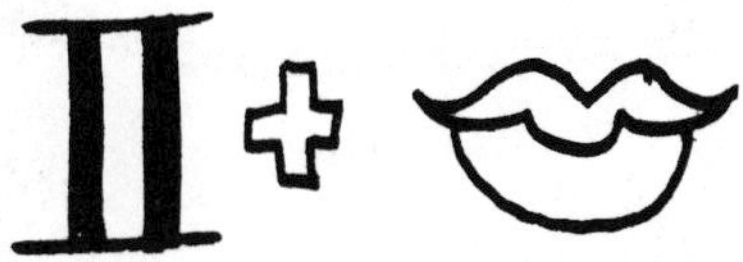
II +

TULIPS (TWO LIPS)

Did Adam and Eve have a date?

no!
N

NO! AN APPLE

MATCH-UPS

MATCH UP THE RIDDLES (ON THIS PAGE) WITH THEIR ANSWERS (THEY'RE OUT OF ORDER) ON THE NEXT PAGE.

1. How many peas are in a pint?

2. What has a center, but no beginning or end?

3. What has teeth, but no mouth?

4. What has a neck, but no head?

5. What tree do you hold in your hand?

A.

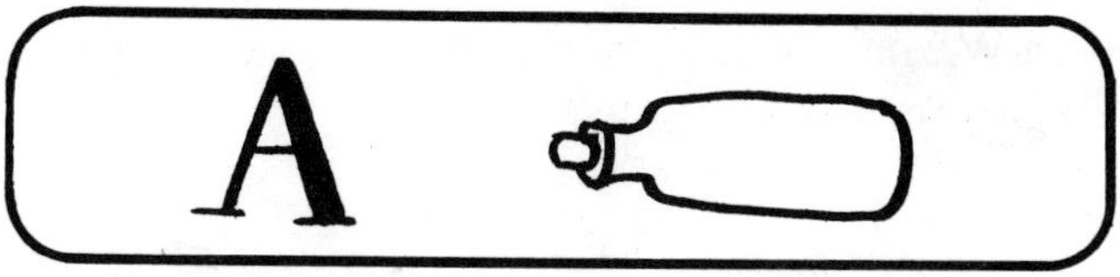
A

B.

C.

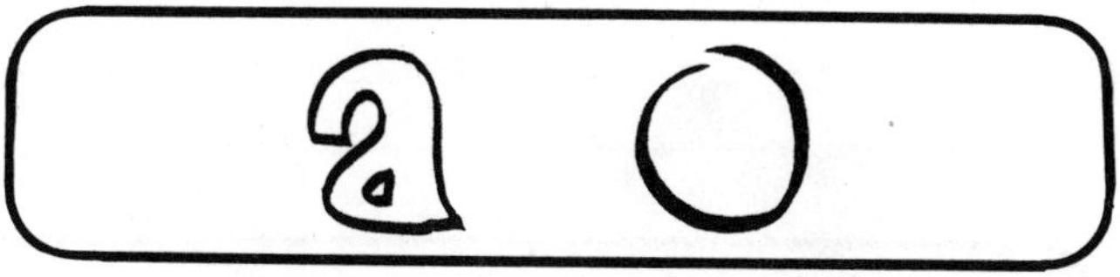
a

D.

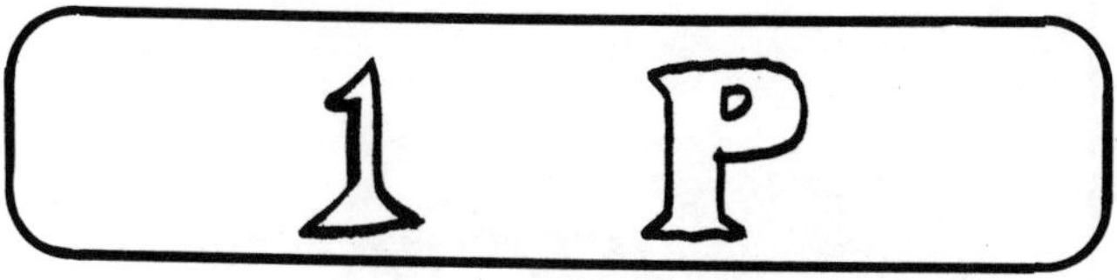
1 P

E.

A

1. ○○○○○○○○○○○○○○○ D (IP) ○○○○○○○○○○○○○○○○
2. ○○○○○○○○○○○○ C (A CIRCLE) ○○○○○○○○○○○○
3. ○○○○○○○○○○○○○ E (A COMB) ○○○○○○○○○○○○○
4. ○○○○○○○○○○○○ A (A BOTTLE) ○○○○○○○○○○○○
5. ○○○○○○○○○○○○○ B (PALM) ○○○○○○○○○○○○○

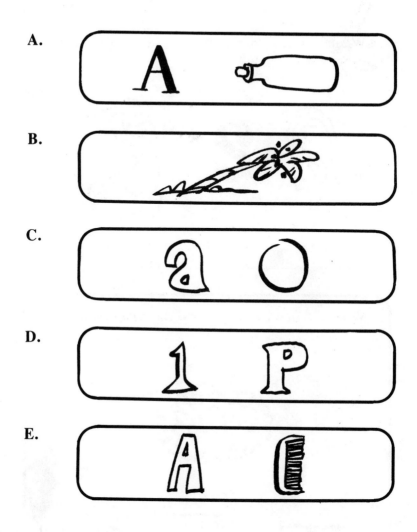

What did the mama broom say to the baby broom at bedtime?

STOP
?
2

"GO TO SWEEP"

What did one banana say to the other banana?

SP +
TO DO
1
2
3
4
- S!

"LET US (LETTUCE) SPLIT!"

What did the mayonnaise say to the refrigerator?

Shut
THE
I'M
+ing

OOOOO "SHUTOTHEODOOR—I'MODRESSING!" OOOO

What baby is born with whiskers?

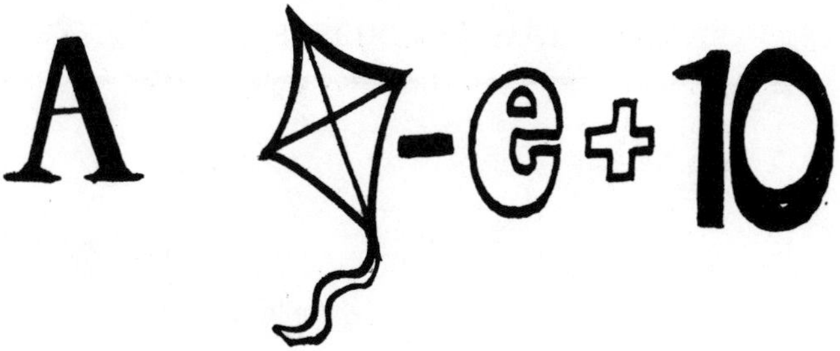
A
-e+10

OOOOOOOOOOOOOOO AOKITTEN OOOOOOOOOOOOOOO

Why did the ocean roar?

Its
SOAP
-H
wet

OOOOOOOOOOOO ITS○BED○WAS○WET OOOOOOOOOOO

HORSE LAUGHS

2.

What do you do at a dude ranch?

art
1lb
-P

OOOOOOOOOOOO HORSEOAROUND OOOOOOOOOOOOO

What do you say to greet a cow?

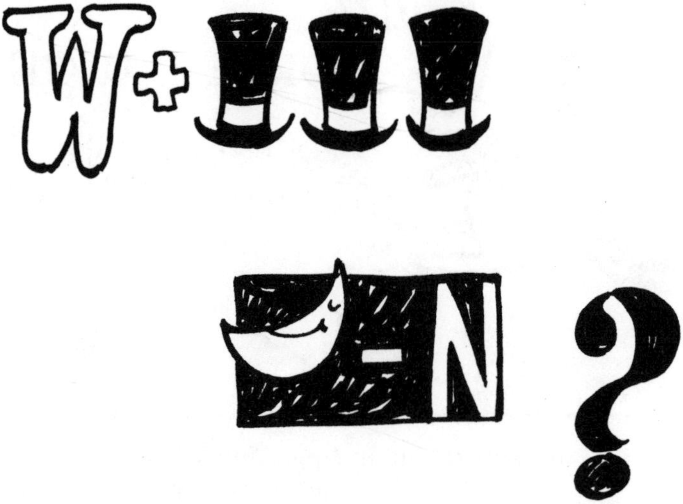

"WHAT'S MOO?"

Why didn't you hear about the 300 cows that disappeared?

nobody's
SANDWICH

NOBODY'S HEARD (HERD)

Why do cows wear bells?

B+
THEIR
DONT
-M+K

○○○ BECAUSE○THEIR○HORNS○DON'T○WORK ○○○

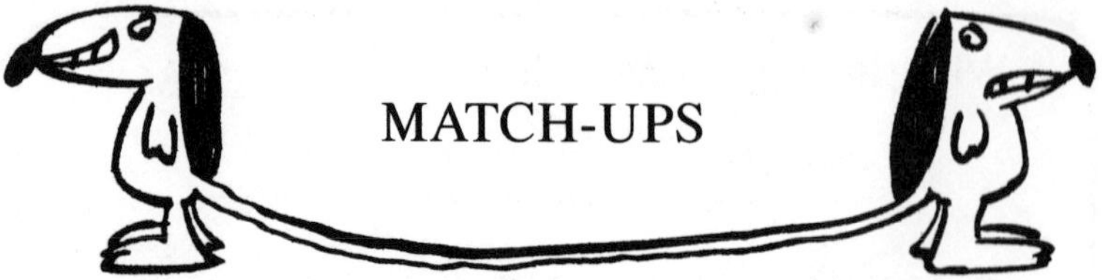

MATCH-UPS

MATCH UP THE RIDDLES (ON THIS PAGE) WITH THEIR ANSWERS (THEY'RE OUT OF ORDER) ON THE NEXT PAGE.

1. Who always goes to sleep with his shoes on?

2. What is as big as a hippopotamus but doesn't weigh an ounce?

3. What weighs almost nothing but cannot be lifted?

4. What runs around the cow pasture but never moves?

5. What makes more noise than a pig caught under a fence?

A.

A
-S

B.

C.

the

D.

a

E.

THE

1. D (A HORSE)
2. C (A HIPPOPOTAMUS'S SHADOW)
3. A (A BUBBLE)
4. E (THE FENCE)
5. B (TWO PIGS CAUGHT UNDER A FENCE)

Why did the horse sneeze?

It
-t+d
a
LITTLE
-D+T

○○○○○ IT○HAD○A○LITTLE○COLT○(COLD) ○○○○○

GOOD DAYS—BAD DAYS

3.

What do insects do on Sunday?

GO 4 a
+GY
ride

○○○○○○○○ GO○FOR○A○BUGGY○RIDE ○○○○○○○○

What should you feed an elephant on?

222
+ DAYS

TUESDAYS (2's DAYS)

What's the best day for making pancakes?

+
DAY

FRIDAY (FRY-DAY)

What did the calculator say to the math teacher?

U
CAN
1 2 3 4
5 6 7 8 9
10 11 12
ON
ME

"YOU CAN COUNT ON ME!"

Where do you put money for a rainy day?

N
a
-r+k

IN A CLOUD BANK

HOW'S BUSINESS?

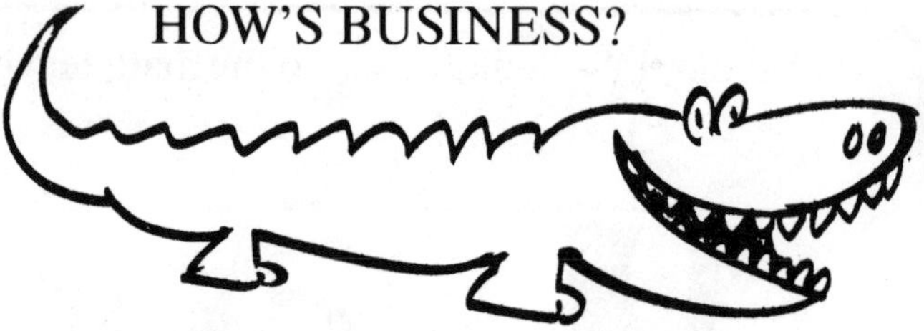

THIS IS A MATCH-UP. JUST PUT THE RIDDLES (ON THIS PAGE) TOGETHER WITH THE BEST ANSWERS (THEY'RE OUT OF ORDER) ON THE NEXT PAGE.

1. How is the astronomy business?

2. How is the electric light business?

3. How is the dress-making business?

4. How is the rodeo business?

5. How is the submarine business?

A.

GOING
-S+DER

B.

OFF

C.

L+
-B+ing
-C

D.

E.

ON
?
&
OFF
?

1. C (LOOKING UP)
2. E (OFF AND ON)
3. D (SEW-SEW) (SO-SO)
4. B (FALLING OFF)
5. A (GOING UNDER)

What did Mrs. Claus say to Santa when she heard a patter on the roof?

it
SOUNDS
L+
-B
,

○ " IT○SOUNDS○LIKE○RAIN,○DEAR○(REINDEER) " ○

SLURPS & BURPS

4.

What's worse than finding a worm in the apple you're eating?

FiND
+
-K
1/2
a

OOOOOOOO FINDINGOHALFOAOWORM OOOOOOOO

What looks like half a pumpkin?

THE
-m
½

THE OTHER HALF

What has hands but never washes them?

a
C+

A CLOCK

What's useless unless it's in a tight spot?

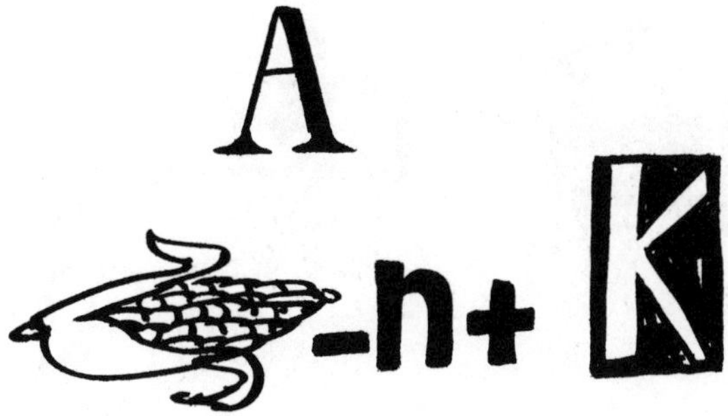

A CORK

What is purple or white and has its heart in its head?

A CABBAGE

What always gets served but never gets eaten?

10 + NIS

TENNIS BALLS

How do you make a lemon drop?

-TER
IT

LET IT FALL

How do you eat soup with a fork?

VERY
SL+
- B+LY

VERY SLOWLY

What cranky violinist do you find on the beach?

A
+r

A FIDDLER CRAB

CRAZY QUESTIONS

1. Why does  shock people?
2. How can you recognize  stew?
3. How do you scold an  ?
4. What did the sugar say to the  ?
5. Why was the  running along the cereal box?

IN A CRAZY QUESTION THE RIDDLE HAS A PICTURE IN IT. YOU NEED TO FIGURE OUT THE RIDDLE QUESTION FIRST AND THEN MATCH IT UP WITH THE ANSWERS (THAT ARE ALL OUT OF ORDER) BELOW.

A. Say "Tusk-Tusk!"

B. It said, "Tear along the dotted line."

C. "I'm sweet, but don't stir me up!"

D. It doesn't know how to conduct itself.

E. By the hares in it.

1. OO D (IT DOESN'T KNOW HOW TO CONDUCT ITSELF) OO
2. OOOOOOOO E (BY THE HARES IN IT) OOOOOOOO
3. OOOOOOO A (SAY "TUSK-TUSK!") OOOOOOO
4. O C ("I'M SWEET, BUT DON'T STIR ME UP!") O
5. O B (IT SAID, "TEAR ALONG THE DOTTED LINE.") O

When is it polite to serve milk in a saucer?

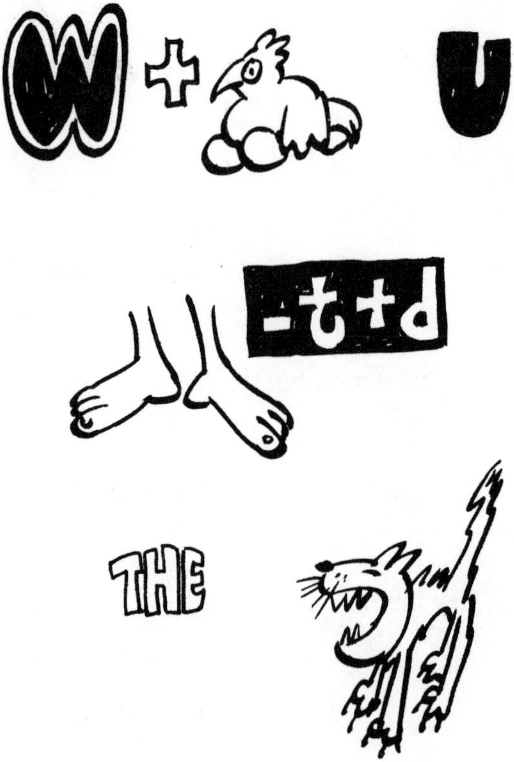
W
U
THE

OOOOOOO WHENOYOUOFEEDOTHEOCAT OOOOOOO

SNEEZES & WHEEZES

5.

If your nose runs and your feet smell, what's wrong with you?

Ur
bt
Q
SIDE

OOOOOO YOU'REBUILTUPSIDEDOWN OOOOOO

What letter can make you sick?

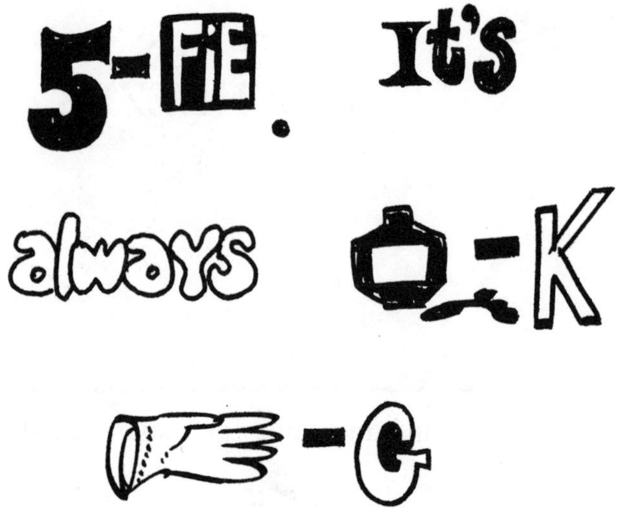
5-FiE
It's
always
-K
-G

OOOOOOO V. O IT'S O ALWAYS O IN O LOVE OOOOOOO

What is a sure cure for dandruff?

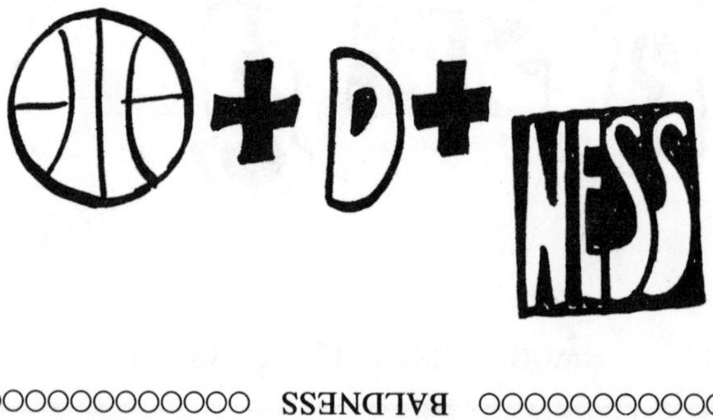
+D+
NESS

OOOOOOOOOOOOOO BALDNESS OOOOOOOOOOOOOO

How can you stop a sleepwalker from walking in his sleep?

+
HiM
aw
+
-SN

KEEP HIM AWAKE

How can you go ten days without sleep and not be tired?

ZZZZ
N+
-L

SLEEP NIGHTS

MATCH-UPS

MATCH UP THE RIDDLES (ON THIS PAGE) WITH THEIR ANSWERS (THEY'RE OUT OF ORDER) ON THE NEXT PAGE.

1. What has pains but no aches?

2. What has a head, and four legs, but only one foot?

3. What can a man be that a woman can't?

4. What never blinks when you stick something in its eye?

5. What has a head and a tail, but no body?

A.

B.

C.

D.

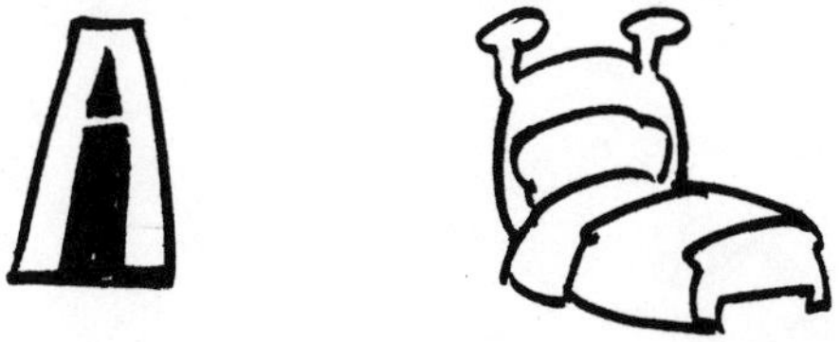

E.

1. B (A WINDOW)
2. D (A BED)
3. E (A FATHER)
4. C (A NEEDLE)
5. A (A COIN)

How do you drive a baby buggy?

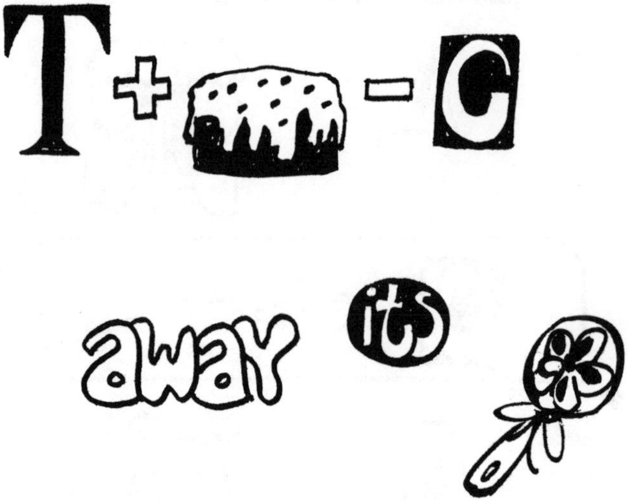
T + − C
away
its

○○○○○○○○ TAKE○AWAY○ITS○RATTLE ○○○○○○○○

If your nose was on strike, what would you do?

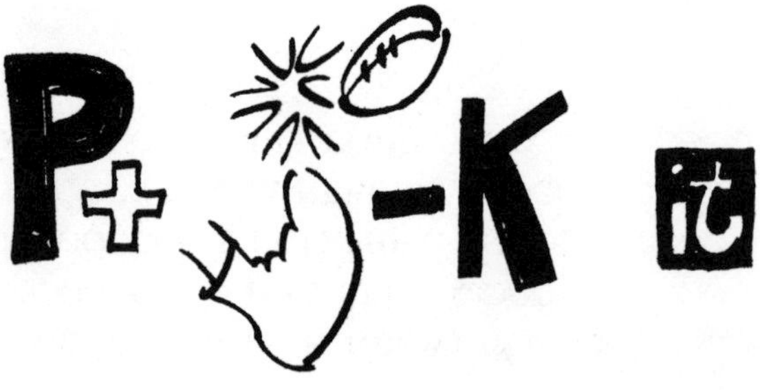
P + −K
it

○○○○○○○○○○○○○ PICKET○(PICK○IT) ○○○○○○○○○○

FOWL PLAY

6.

What did the baby chick say when the hen laid an orange?

O, C THE
MAR+
ma
+ laid!

"OH, SEE THE ORANGE MARMALADE (LAID)!"

What bird looks most like a stork?

+
-M

ANOTHER STORK

How can you keep a rooster from crowing on Monday?

HiM
ON
+ DAY

EAT HIM ON SUNDAY

What did the chicken say to the rooster?

LET
me
-B+E
Ur

"LET ME USE YOUR COMB"

What happened when the hen swallowed a yo-yo?

she
L+
-M
THE
SAME
3X

SHE LAID THE SAME EGG THREE TIMES

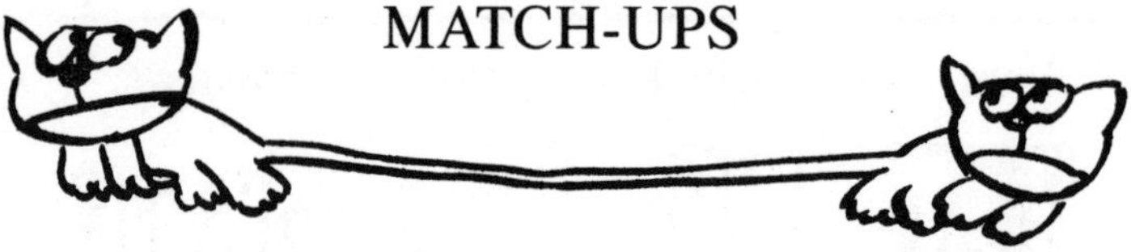

MATCH-UPS

MATCH UP THE RIDDLES (ON THIS PAGE) WITH THEIR ANSWERS (THEY'RE OUT OF ORDER) ON THE NEXT PAGE.

1. Where do giant condors come from?
2. If an egg comes floating down the river, where does it come from?
3. What becomes more valuable when it's used up?
4. What grows up as it grows down?
5. What's the best thing for hives?

A.

A

B.

BBBBB

C.

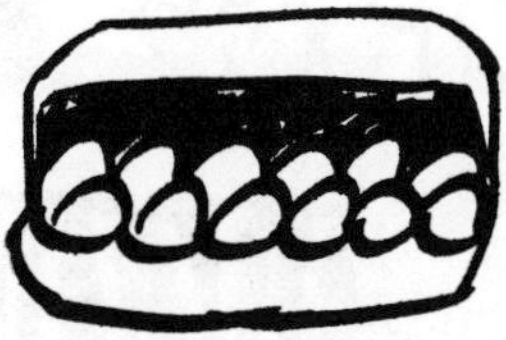

D.

a

E.

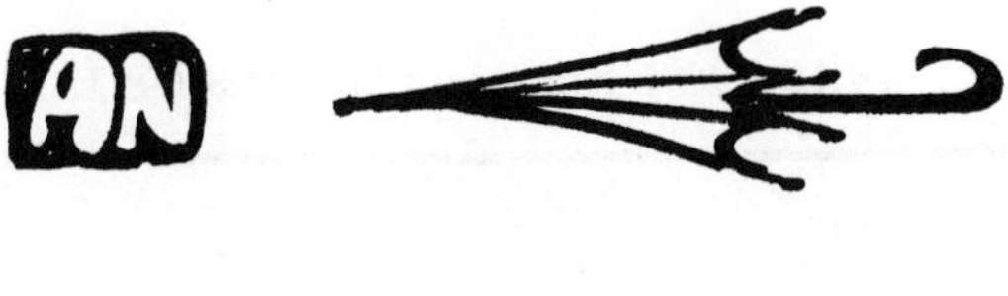
AN

1. ○○○○○○○○○○○○○ C (EGGS) ○○○○○○○○○○○○○○
2. ○○○○○○○○○○○ D (A CHICKEN) ○○○○○○○○○○○○
3. ○○○○○○○○○ E (AN UMBRELLA) ○○○○○○○○○○○
4. ○○○○○○○○○○○○ A (A GOOSE) ○○○○○○○○○○○○
5. ○○○○○○○○○○○○○ B (BEES) ○○○○○○○○○○○○○○

Why does a chicken lay an egg?

If
-EP
DROPPED
it
, it
WOULD
br+
-C

IF SHE DROPPED IT, IT WOULD BREAK

MOVING RIGHT ALONG . . .

7.

What has three feet but can't walk?

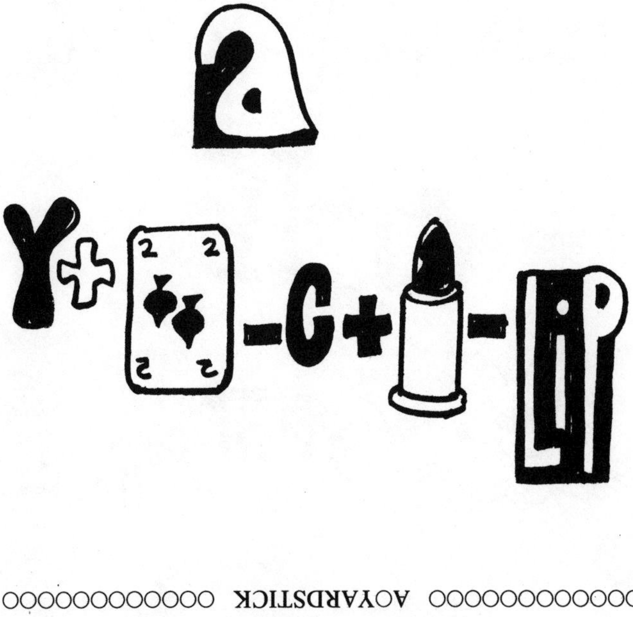

Y + − C + − LIP

OOOOOOOOOOOO AOYARDSTICK OOOOOOOOOOOOO

What part of New York is in Chicago?

the

THE LETTER O

How can you make O move?

PUT
a
10.00
-TA
-K
-G+NT
OF
IT

PUT A GO IN FRONT OF IT

What is the hardest key to turn?

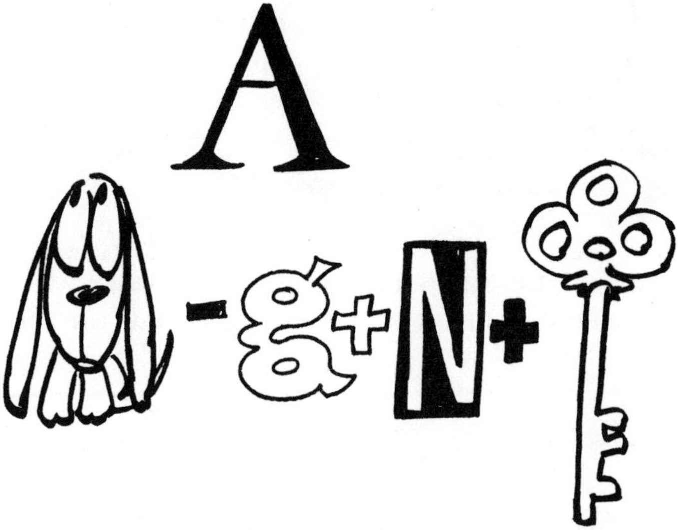
A
- g + N +

A DONKEY

What has sleeves and is put on wet?

A
OF

A COAT OF PAINT

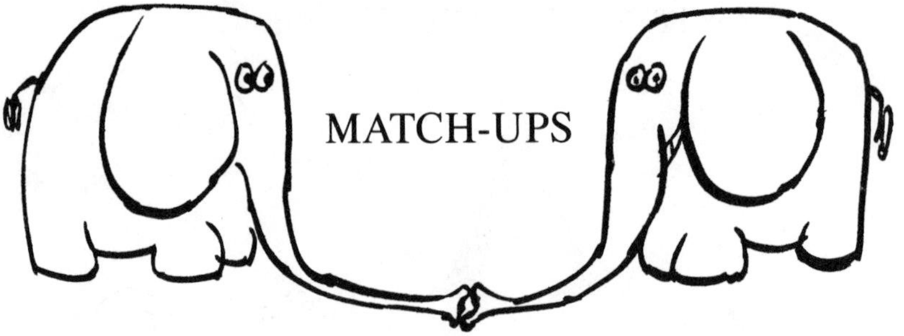

MATCH-UPS

MATCH UP THE RIDDLES (ON THIS PAGE) WITH THEIR ANSWERS (THEY'RE OUT OF ORDER) ON THE NEXT PAGE.

1. What kind of room has no walls?

2. What always enters the house through the keyhole?

3. What is both inside and outside the house—yet in its place?

4. The English alphabet goes from A to Z. What goes from Z to A?

5. What does a poor man have—that a rich man wants?

A.

O

B.

The

C.

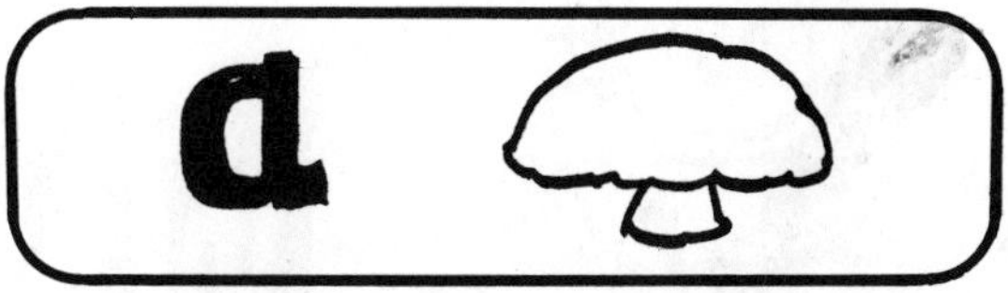
a

D.

the

E.

a

1. OOOOOOOOOO C (A MUSHROOM) OOOOOOOOOO
2. OOOOOOOOOOOO D (THE KEY) OOOOOOOOOOOO
3. OOOOOOOOOOO B (THE DOOR) OOOOOOOOOOO
4. OOOOOOOOOOOO E (A ZEBRA) OOOOOOOOOOOO
5. OOOOOOOOOOOO A (NOTHING) OOOOOOOOOOOO

When General Lee fell off his horse, which way was he going?

D+
-G+
WN

OOOOOOOOOOOOOOOO DOWN OOOOOOOOOOOOOOOO

How do you get from here to there?

$$\begin{array}{r} 1 \\ +2 \\ +3 \\ +2 \\ \hline =8 \end{array}$$

T

OOOOOOOOOOOOOOOO ADDOT OOOOOOOOOOOOOOOO

I never ask questions, but I demand many answers. What am I?

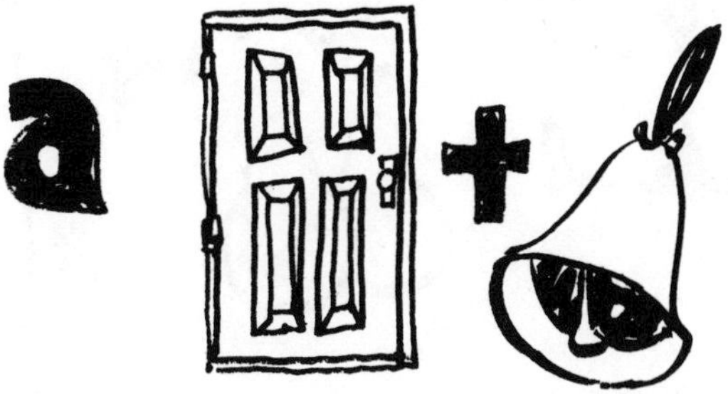

A DOORBELL

Where was Noah when the lights went out?

N
the
D+

IN THE DARK

What has a hundred legs, but can't walk?

50
OF

50 PAIRS OF PANTS

What runs in and out of town—day and night?

THE
I AM NOT A FROG

THE ROAD

Why is a large coat like a banana peel?

they r
- A + H
e z 2
S + - G ON

○○○ THEY○ARE○BOTH○EASY○TO○SLIP○ON ○○○

What was the turtle doing on the freeway?

½ a
-K+e
aN hour

OOOOOOOO HALFOAOMILEOANOHOUR OOOOOOOO

BAD LUCK!

8.

How do you keep a skunk from smelling?

H
its

○○○○○○○○○○○ HOLD○ITS○NOSE ○○○○○○○○○○○

What do you get if you cross a skunk and a porcupine?

A

SNIFF
SNIFF
PHEW!
+ Y

OOOOOOOO AOSMELLYOPINCUSHION OOOOOOOO

How did the mouse get a short tail?

+ NiP

OOOOOOOOOOOOOOOO CATNIP OOOOOOOOOOOOOOOO

When the dinosaur fell in the swimming pool, how did it get out?

W
VS

WET

What has 50 heads, but no brains?

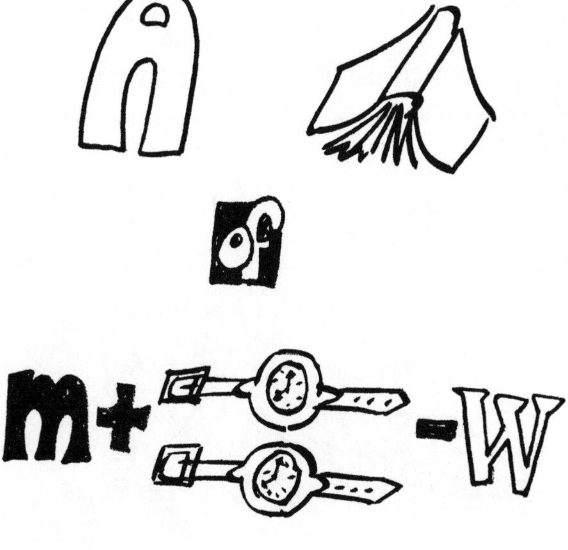
of
m
W

A BOOK OF MATCHES

What makes the cemetery so noisy?

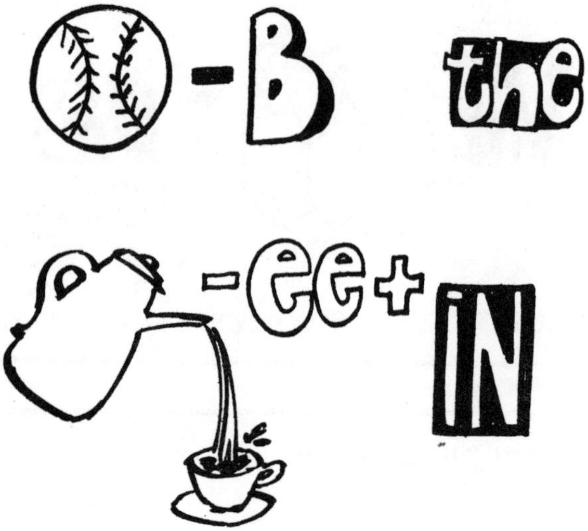
-B
the
-ee+
iN

ALL THE COUGHIN' (COFFIN)

Why are banks noisy?

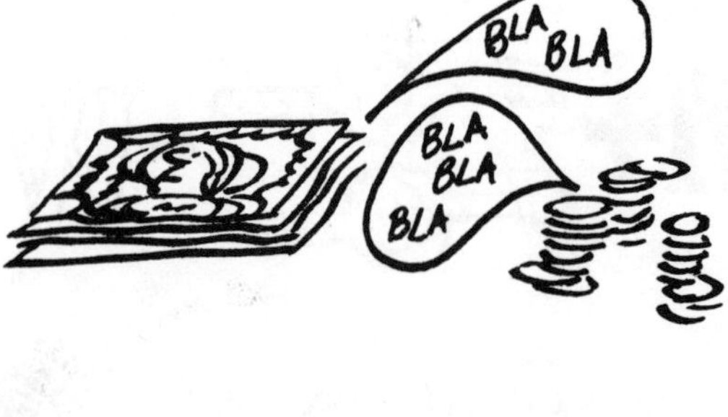
BLA BLA
BLA
BLA
BLA

MONEY TALKS

What has two tongues and no mouth?

A
of

A PAIR OF SHOES

When is it good to lose your temper?

W+
its
A
-L
1

WHEN IT'S A BAD ONE

CRAZY QUESTIONS

1. Why was the mother  sad?

SCRATCH
SCRATCH

2. What kind of  makes you move faster?

3. What goes from New York to iANROFiLAC without moving?

4. What's worse than raining  and  ?

5. Where do you find  ?

IN A CRAZY QUESTION THE RIDDLE HAS A PICTURE IN IT. YOU NEED TO FIGURE OUT THE RIDDLE QUESTION FIRST AND THEN MATCH IT UP WITH THE ANSWERS (THAT ARE ALL OUT OF ORDER) BELOW.

A. Hailing buses.

B. Railroad tracks.

C. Where you lost them.

D. All her children had gone to the dogs.

E. A hurricane.

1. OO FLEA—D (ALL HER CHILDREN HAD GONE OO
OOOOOOOOOOOO TO THE DOGS) OOOOOOOOOOOOO
2. OOOOOOOO CANE—E (A HURRICANE) OOOOOOOO
3. OOOO CALIFORNIA—B (RAILROAD TRACKS) OOOO
4. OOOOO CATS/DOGS—A (HAILING BUSES) OOOOO
5. OOOO TIGERS—C (WHERE YOU LOST THEM) OOOO

What must an astronaut do before he gets out of his space suit?

g+
-h
N2 it

OOOOOOOOOOOOOO GETOINTOIT OOOOOOOOOOOO

Why shouldn't you swim on an empty stomach?

It'S
-P+
ier
N

OOOOOOOOO IT'SOEASIEROINOWATER OOOOOOOOO

When is a donkey not a donkey?

W +
it's
a
- er + le

WHEN IT'S A LITTLE HOARSE (HORSE)

Why did Myrtle wave her hair?

She
DiDN'T
½
a

SHE DIDN'T HAVE A FLAG

FUN & GAMES

9.

What did the mad magician pull out of his hat?

HIS
DON'T CALL ME RABBIT!

HIS HARE (HAIR)

Why do bad mice run faster than good mice?

-N+YS
+
-F
-GS+T

○○○○○ MICE○(NICE)○GUYS○FINISH○LAST ○○○○○

When mice go jogging, what do they wear?

SQ+
-SN

SQUEAKERS (SNEAKERS)

Why is R always a winner?

It's
-LT+
WAYS
1ST
N
a
r+
A

IT'S ALWAYS FIRST IN A RACE

What kind of paper makes the best kite?

PA+
-a

FLY PAPER

Why did the baseball coach put a spider on the team?

2
+CH

TO CATCH FLIES

What can you hold in your left hand but not in your right?

Ur
R + - L
L +

YOUR○RIGHT○ELBOW

Can you row?

S,
+ ?

YES,○CAN○YOU○(CANOE)?

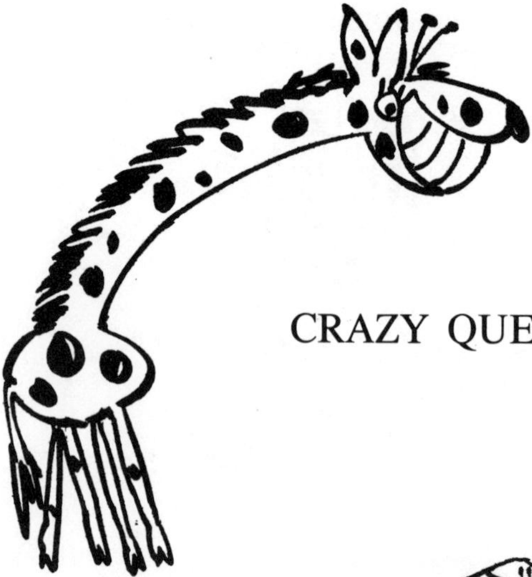

CRAZY QUESTIONS

1. Did you ever see a  bake?

2. Did you ever see a  drawer?

3. Did you ever see a  shake?

4. Did you ever see a  smoke?

5. Did you ever see a  punch?

IN A CRAZY QUESTION THE RIDDLE HAS A PICTURE IN IT. YOU NEED TO FIGURE OUT THE RIDDLE QUESTION FIRST AND THEN MATCH IT UP WITH THE ANSWERS (THAT ARE ALL OUT OF ORDER) BELOW.

A. No, but I've seen an engine puff.

B. No, but I've seen an apple turnover.

C. No, but I've seen a base hit.

D. No, but I've seen greasepaint.

E. No, but I've seen an oyster stew.

1. OOOO CLAM—E(NO,BUTI'VESEENAN OOOO
OOOOOOOOOOO OYSTERSTEW)OOOOOOOOOOOOO
2. OOOO DRESSER—D(NO,BUTI'VESEEN OOOOO
OOOOOOOOOOO GREASEPAINT) OOOOOOOOOOOOO
3. O STRAWBERRY—B(NO,BUTI'VESEENAN OO
OOOOOOOOOO APPLETURNOVER) OOOOOOOOOOO
4. OOO CHIMNEY—A(NO,BUTI'VESEENAN OOO
OOOOOOOOOOO ENGINEPUFF) OOOOOOOOOOOOO
5. OOOOO FRUIT—C(NO,BUTI'VESEENAOOOOO
OOOOOOOOOOOOO BASEHIT) OOOOOOOOOOOOOO

How did the girl octopus and the boy octopus come aboard Noah's Ark?

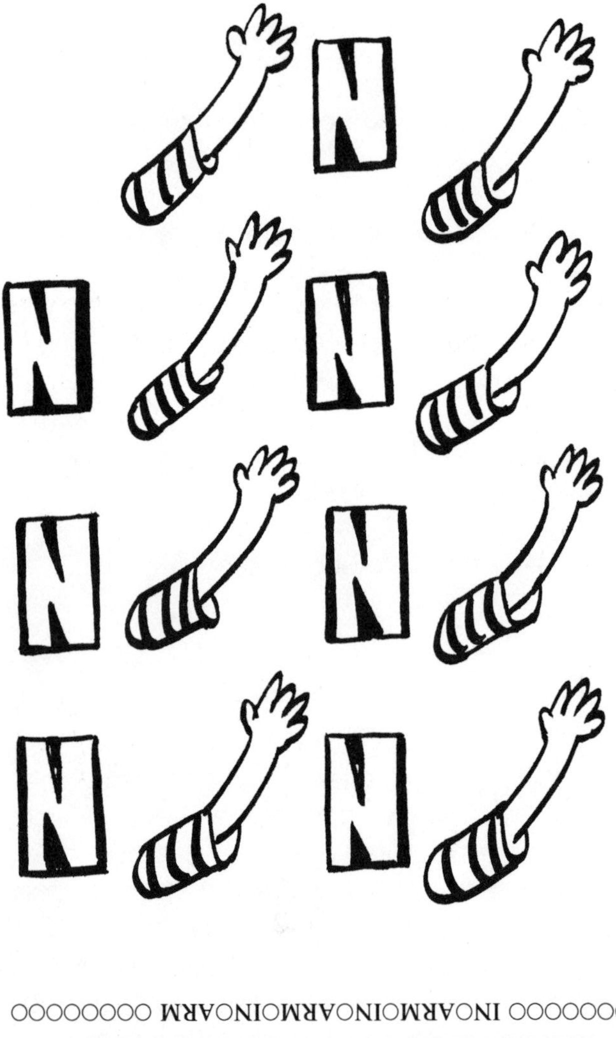

OOOOOOOO INOARMOINOARMOINOARM OOOOOOOO

OO ARMOINOARMOINOARMOINOARMOINOARM OO

PLAYING IT SAFE

10.

What has eight feet, four heads and sings?

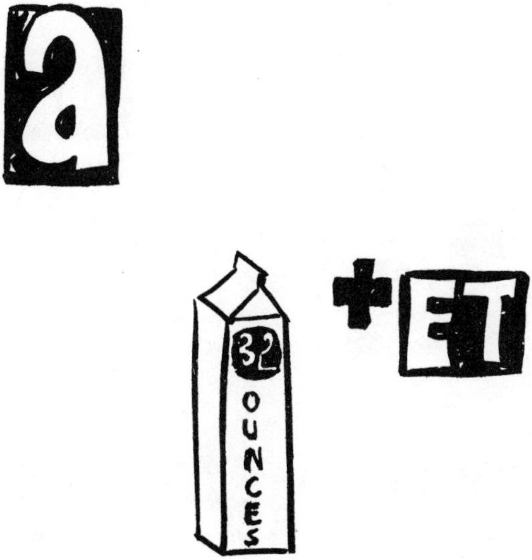
a
32
OUNCES
+ET

A QUARTET

What did the hornplayer say to the drummer?

B+
T!

"BEAT IT!"

What did the drummer say to the hornplayer?

DON'T
G+ -H
a
t+ -h
????

"I DON'T GIVE A HOOT!"

What did the hornplayer say to the violinist?

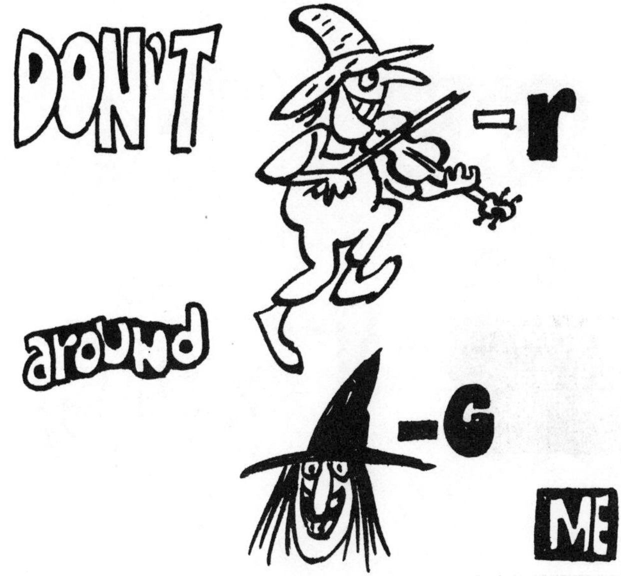
DON'T
-r
around
-G
ME

"DON'T FIDDLE AROUND WITH ME!"

What did the piano player say to the violinist?

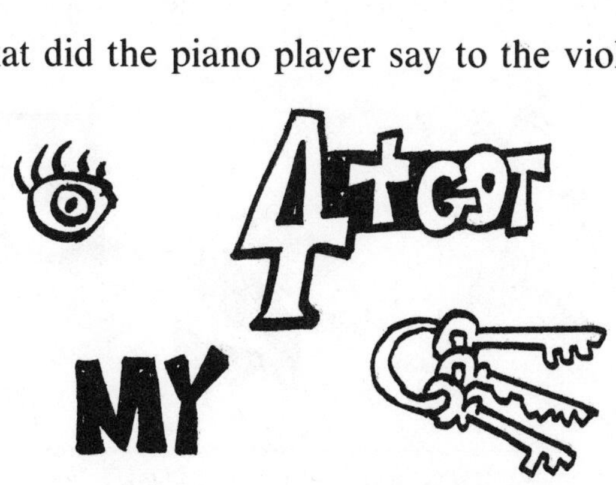
4+GOT
MY

"I FORGOT MY KEYS."

What did the composer say to the harpist?

DON'T
ST+
-N
along

“DON'T STRING ME ALONG!”

What did the harpist say to the composer?

2
U!

“NOTES (NUTS) TO YOU!”

What do you call ten stones with electric guitars?

A
GR...
DOWN

A ROCK GROUP

What kind of musical group makes no sound?

A
B

A RUBBER BAND

CRAZY QUESTIONS

1. Why don't mice answer the  ?

2. How does a  get rid of his customers?

3. How can you  and not get hurt?

4. What did the  sing to the  ?

5. Why did the  spit up Jonah?

IN A CRAZY QUESTION THE RIDDLE HAS A PICTURE IN IT. YOU NEED TO FIGURE OUT THE RIDDLE QUESTION FIRST AND THEN MATCH IT UP WITH THE ANSWERS (THAT ARE ALL OUT OF ORDER) BELOW.

A. "There will never be another ewe."

B. Jump out of a basement window.

C. Because no mews is good mews.

D. You can't keep a good man down.

E. He gives them the brush.

1. ○○ TELEPHONE—C○(BECAUSE○NO○MEWS○IS ○○ ○○○○○○○○○○○○ GOOD○MEWS) ○○○○○○○○○○○○
2. ○ BARBER—E○(HE○GIVES○THEM○THE○BRUSH)
3. ○○○○○ JUMP○OUT○OF○A○WINDOW— ○○○○○○ ○○ B○(JUMP○OUT○OF○A○BASEMENT○WINDOW) ○○
4. ○ BOY○SHEEP/GIRL○SHEEP—A○("THERE○WILL ○ ○○○○○○ NEVER○BE○ANOTHER○EWE") ○○○○○○○
5. ○○○○ WHALE—D○(YOU○CAN'T○KEEP○A ○○○○○ ○○○○○○○○○○○ GOOD○MAN○DOWN) ○○○○○○○○○○○

What do singers always take before singing?

a
-R+P
b+
-W

A DEEP BREATH

CELEBRITY RIDDLES

11.

What game did Dr. Jekyll like to play?

HY+ -er
N

HYDE-AND-SICK (HIDE-AND-SEEK)

What does everyone have that Adam and Eve didn't have?

T

OOOOOOOOOOOOOOOOO PARENTS OOOOOOOOOOOOOO

At what time of day was Adam created?

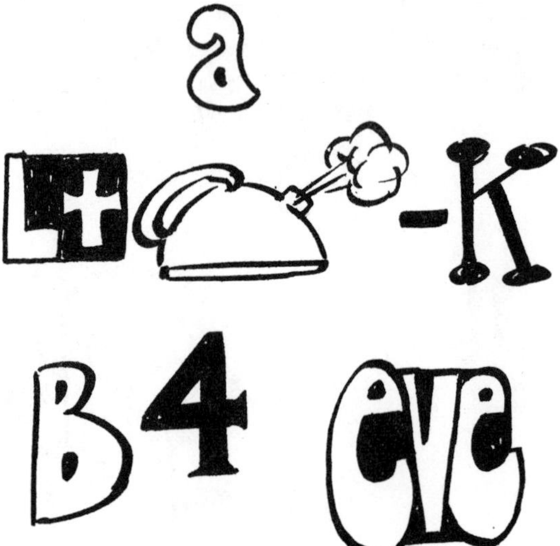
a
L
K
B4 eve

OOOOOOOOO AOLITTLEOBEFOREOEVE OOOOOOOOO

When did queens carry large umbrellas?

W+
+d

WHEN KINGS REIGNED (RAINED)

Where are kings usually crowned?

ON
T+
-N

ON THE HEAD

Why don't radishes disagree with Muhammad Ali?

THEY
WOULDNT
D +
- B

THEY WOULDN'T DARE

Why was Grant buried in Grant's tomb?

HE
SOAP
-H
D+
-BR

○○○○○○○○○○○○○ HE○WAS○DEAD ○○○○○○○○○○○○

What did you see when Merlin set off the fireworks?

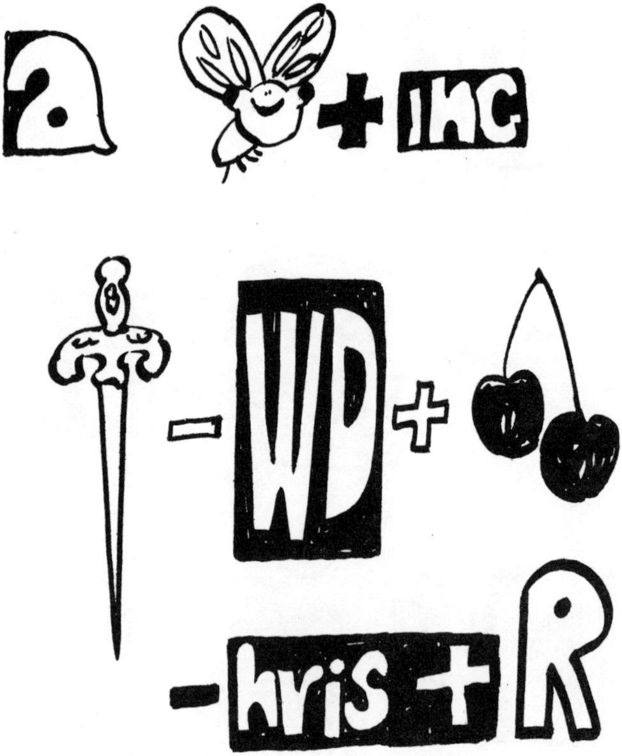
INC
WD
hris
R

OOOOOOOOOOO AOFLYINGOSORCERER OOOOOOOOOOO

HOW BEASTLY!

12.

How can you tell an elephant from an absent-minded professor?

The
REME+
2 7 3
1 5
9 8 4
-NU

THE ELEPHANT REMEMBERS

Why do tigers lie down?

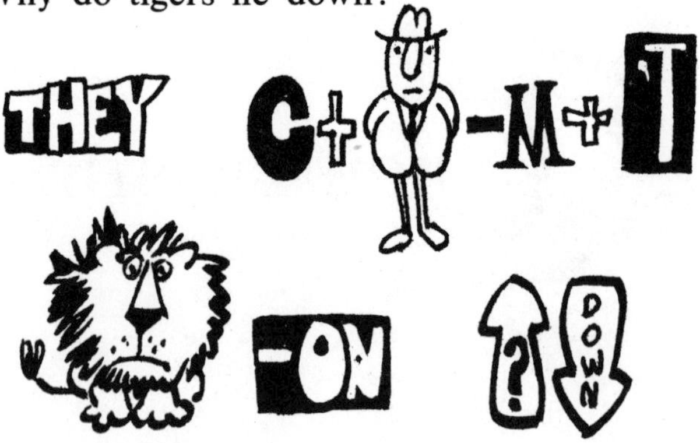
THEY
C+
-M+'T
-ON
?
DOWN

OOOOOOOOOOO THEYOCAN'TOLIEOUP OOOOOOOOOO

Why do tigers eat raw meat?

THEY
C+
-P
C+
-B

OOOOOOOOOOO THEYOCAN'TOCOOK OOOOOOOOOO

Why are leopards spotted?

U
CAN
T+
-B
THEM
-G+M
SCRATCH
SCRATCH

SO YOU CAN TELL THEM FROM FLEAS

What time is it when a monkey scratches a flea?

F+
-H
after
1

FIVE AFTER ONE

How did the gorilla get out of its cage?

WITH
a
+

OOOOO WITH○A○MONKEY○(A○MONK○KEY) OOOOO

What should you do if you find a gorilla asleep in your bed?

ZZZZ
SOMEW+
-B
-BT+SE

OOOOOOOO SLEEP○SOMEWHERE○ELSE OOOOOOOO

Why does a woolly sheep scratch himself?

HE
-T
-Y+ EECE

OOOOOOOO HEOHASOFLEASO(FLEECE) OOOOOOOO

On which side does a bear have fur?

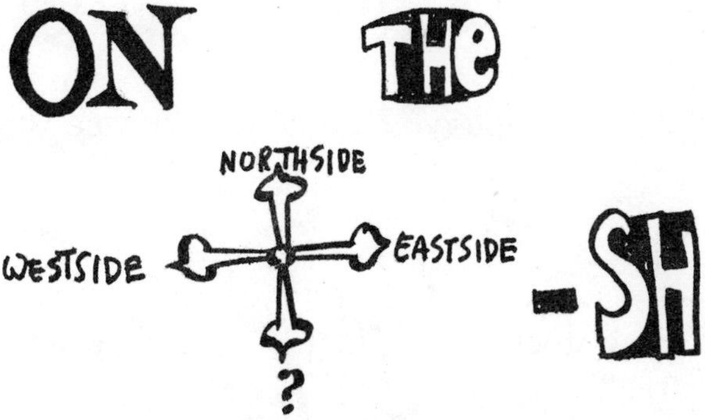
ON
THE
NORTHSIDE
WESTSIDE
EASTSIDE
?
-SH

OOOOOOOOOOOOO ONOTHEOOUTSIDE OOOOOOOOOOOO

CRAZY QUESTIONS

1. How do you get fur from a  ?

2. What did the  say to the  ?

3. When is a  not a  ?

4. What should you do if you see an angry  ?

5. How does an  get up an oak tree?

IN A CRAZY QUESTION THE RIDDLE HAS A PICTURE IN IT. YOU NEED TO FIGURE OUT THE RIDDLE QUESTION FIRST AND THEN MATCH IT UP WITH THE ANSWERS (THAT ARE ALL OUT OF ORDER) BELOW.

A. When it's lion (lying) down.

B. Hope it doesn't see you.

C. "It's been nice gnawing (knowing) you."

D. He climbs on an acorn and waits.

E. Climb a tree.

1. BEAR—E (CLIMB A TREE)
2. BEAVER/TREE—C ("IT'S BEEN NICE GNAWING YOU")
3. TIGER/TIGER—A (WHEN IT'S LION DOWN)
4. RHINOCEROS—B (HOPE IT DOESN'T SEE YOU)
5. ELEPHANT—D (HE CLIMBS ON AN ACORN AND WAITS)

What did Papa Gnu say to Mama Gnu when Baby Gnu was naughty?

-at
Ur
-L+N
GNU

OOOOO "GO○PADDLE○YOUR○OWN○GNU" OOOOOO

MAD MENAGERIE

13.

What does a farmer say when you tell him a joke?

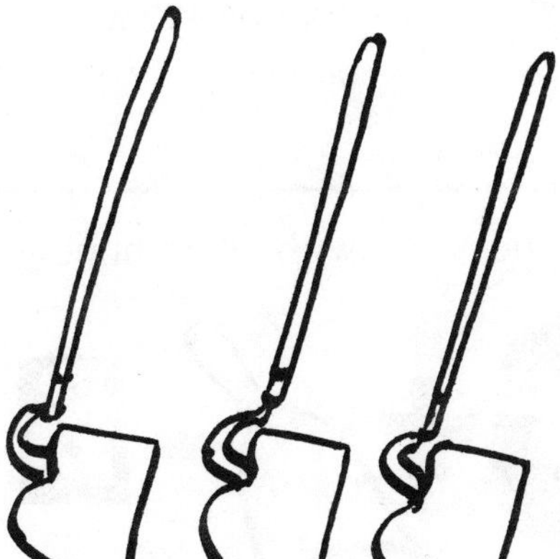

HO-HO-HO (HOE-HOE-HOE)

How do pigs write?

– C
A
+

WITH A PIG PEN

What do bees do with their honey?

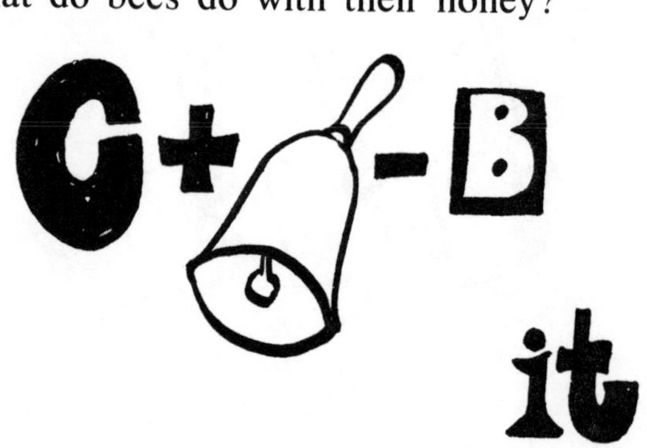
C + – B
it

CELL IT (SELL IT)

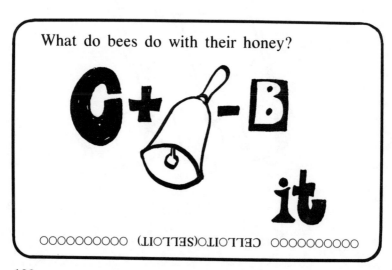

How do you make wild corn behave?

its

OOOOOOOOOOOOO BOX○ITS○EARS OOOOOOOOOOOO

Where do little ears of corn come from?

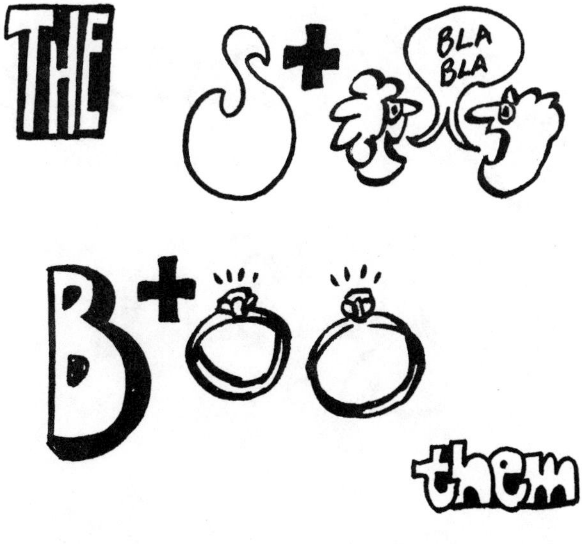
THE
BLA
BLA
B
them

OOOO THE○STORK○(STALK)○BRINGS○THEM OOOO

Why did the farmer stand behind the donkey?

-N
THOUGHT
-A
GET
a
-mh
IT

HE THOUGHT HE'D GET A KICK
OUT OF IT

Why don't farmers milk their mice?

they
C+
-P
G+
-a
THE
OVER
AND
?
+neath

○○ THEY○CAN'T○GET○TO○THE○PAIL○UNDERNEATH ○

Why is a goose like a cow's tail?

THEY
B+
-to
GR-R-
OW
DOWN

THEY BOTH GROW DOWN

What is smaller than a flea's mouth?

A
fl+
-r

A FLEA'S LIPS

What did the dog do at the flea circus?

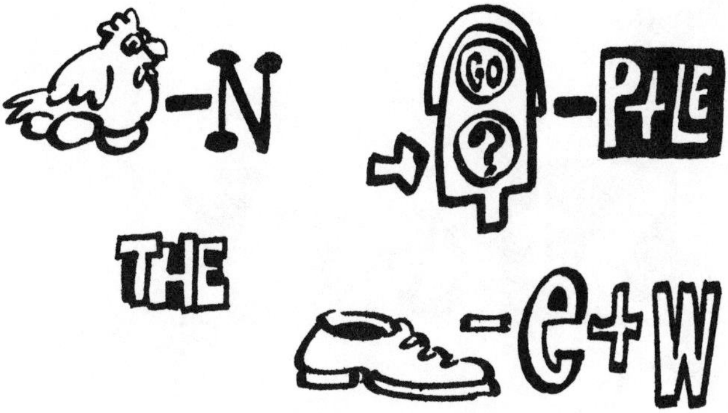
-N
GO
?
-P+LE
THE
-e+W

HE STOLE THE SHOW

Why does a dog wag his tail?

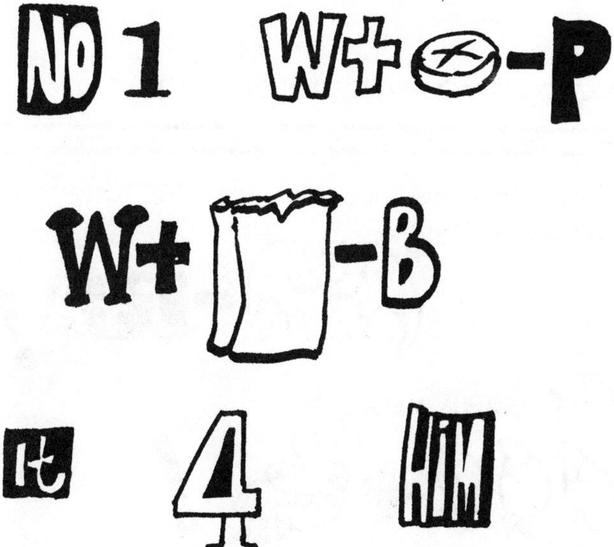
NO 1
W+
-P
W+
-B
it
4
HIM

NO ONE WILL WAG IT FOR HIM

What did the cat see in the desert on Christmas Eve?

St &+y

OOOOOO SANDYCLAWS (SANTACLAUS) OOOOOO

What did the bee say to the sheep on Christmas Day?

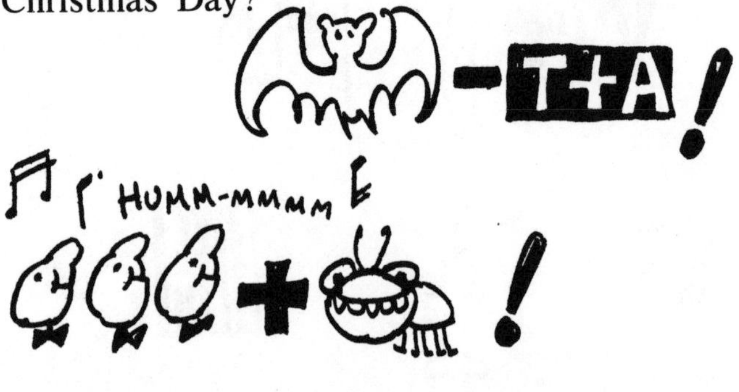
-T+A!
HUMM-MMMM

OOOOOOOOOOO "BAH! HUMBUG!" OOOOOOOOOOO

Why is a cat on a fence like a coin?

It
-ND
on
1
-L,
on
the

IT HAS A HEAD ON ONE SIDE, TAIL ON THE OTHER

What has four heads, four tails and smells?

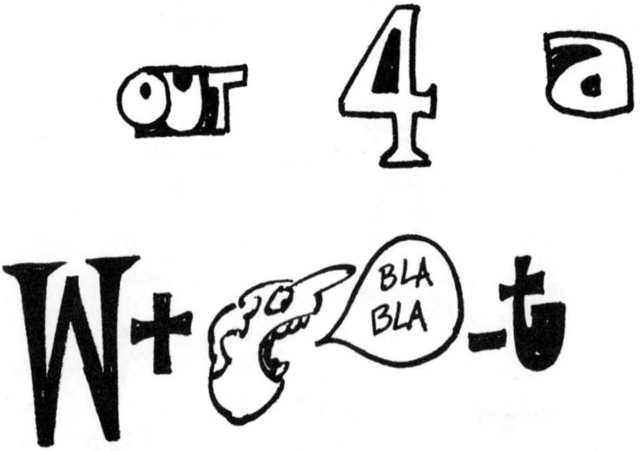
OUT
4
a
W+
BLA
BLA
-t

FOUR DOGS OUT FOR A WALK

GRAB BAG

14.

What does someone else have to take before you get it?

UR

YOUR PICTURE

How do you make a cigarette lighter?

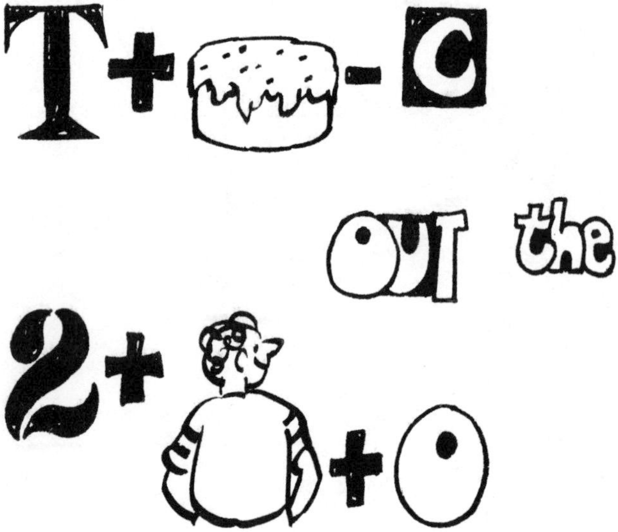
T + − C
OUT the
2 + + O

oooooooo TAKE o OUT o THE o TOBACCO oooooooo

What can write blue, red, green, orange, yellow and black?

A
+ CIL

ooooooooooooooo A o PENCIL oooooooooooooo

What can you give someone and still keep?

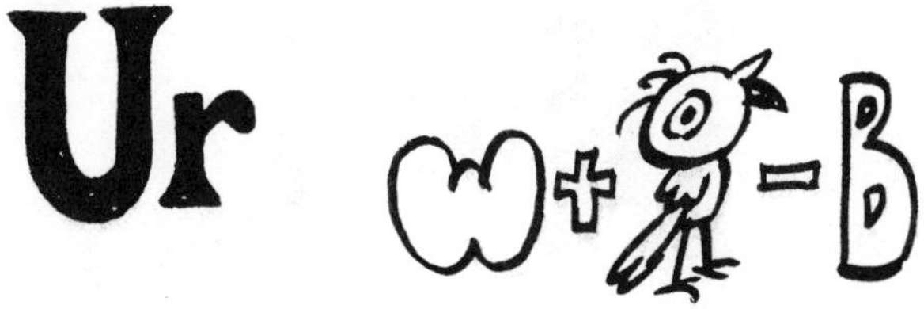
Ur
W + -B

YOUR WORD

What can you break with one word?

SiL+
-f

SILENCE

How much dirt is there in a hole two feet deep and one foot across?

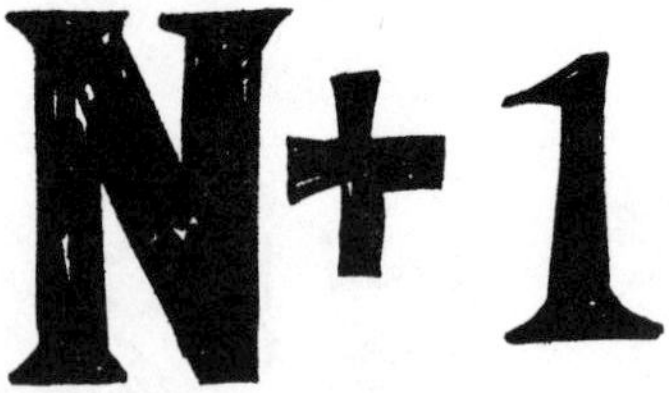
N+1

OOOOOOOOOOOOOOOO NONE OOOOOOOOOOOOOOOO

What falls down all the time, but never gets hurt?

A

OOOOOOOOOOOO A WATERFALL OOOOOOOOOOOO

How do you turn a 30-piece set of dishes into a 300-piece set?

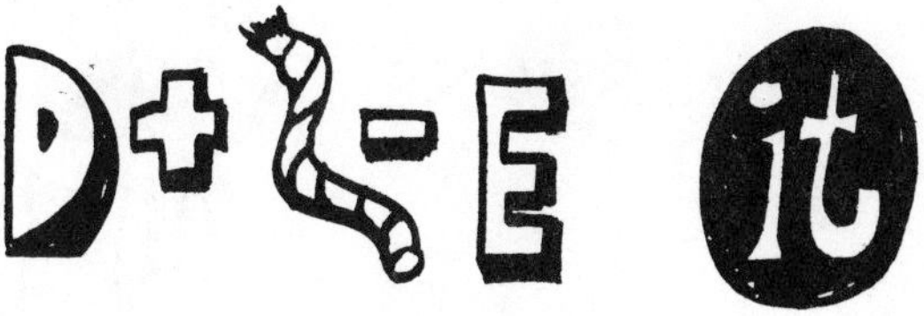

DROPIT

What happens if the rain keeps up?

IT WON'T COME DOWN

CRAZY QUESTIONS

1. What has a  but never speaks and a bed but never  ?

2. What kind of  do you use in math class?

3. Why couldn't they play cards on the  ?
NOAH

4. Why do you put the right  on first?

5. What did the  say to the jeweler?

IN A CRAZY QUESTION THE RIDDLE HAS A PICTURE IN IT. YOU NEED TO FIGURE OUT THE RIDDLE QUESTION FIRST AND THEN MATCH IT UP WITH THE ANSWERS (THAT ARE ALL OUT OF ORDER) BELOW.

A. It's silly to put on the wrong one.

B. "Give me a ring sometime."

C. A river.

D. Because Noah sat on the deck.

E. Multipliers.

1. MOUTH/SLEEPS—C (A RIVER)
2. PLIERS—E (MULTIPLIERS)
3. ARK—D (BECAUSE NOAH SAT ON THE DECK)
4. SHOE—A (IT'S SILLY TO PUT ON THE WRONG ONE)
5. BATHTUB—B ("GIVE ME A RING SOMETIME.")

If Harold wears his pants out before noon, what should he do?

W
+
THEM
N

WEAR THEM BACK IN

TOUGHIES

15.

Why do white sheep eat more than black sheep?

THERE
r
mt
-C
of
them

OOOOOOO THERE ARE MORE OF THEM OOOOOOO

What did the dandelion say to the flower bed?

T+
-G
me 2
uR
-HL+
DER

○○○○○○○ TAKE○ME○TO○YOUR○WEEDER ○○○○○○○

Would you help a lady in distress?

'D
SL+P
a
Ne

○○○○○ I'D○HELP○A○LADY○IN○ANY○DRESS ○○○○○

What did the big toe say to the little toe?

THERE'S
a
-W
foL +
-T
us

OOOOO "THERE'SOAOHEELOFOLLOWINGOUS" OOOOO

When does a horse see as much from behind as in front?

WHEN
its
r

○○○○○○ WHEN○ITS○EYES○ARE○CLOSED ○○○○○○

Why does a dog chase its tail?

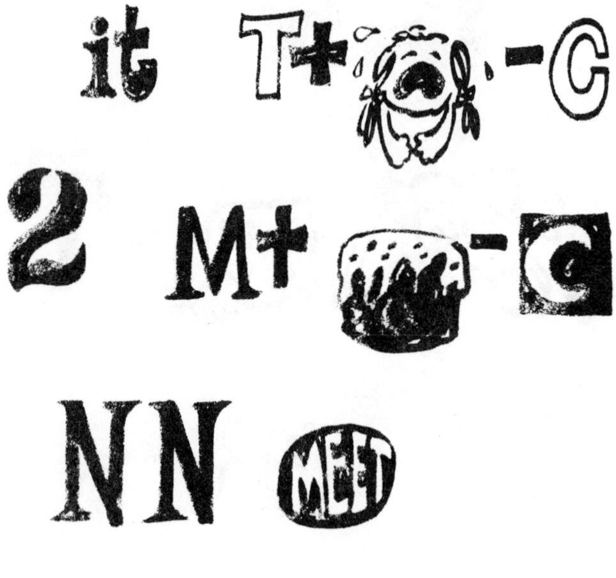
it
2
NN
MEET

○○○○ IT○TRIES○TO○MAKE○ENDS○(NNs)○MEET ○○○○

How can you swallow a door without choking?

B+
-GA+T
it
D+
-CL

BOLT IT DOWN

Which snake is best at arithmetic?

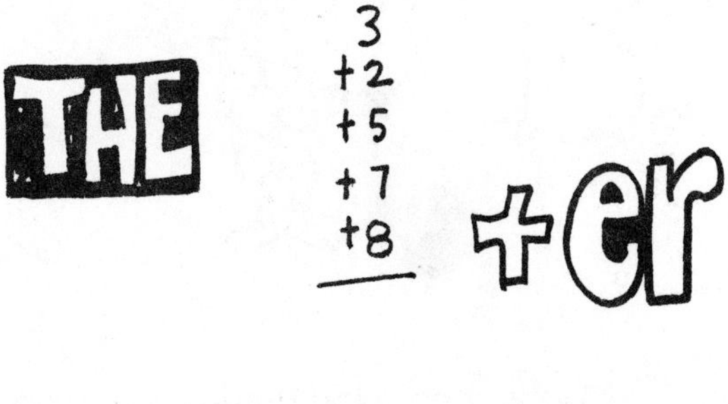
THE
3
+2
+5
+7
+8
+er

THE ADDER

Why was the baby goat angry at its parents?

T + - h + y
- e + - SK + D
it L + - B
a

THEY TREATED IT LIKE A KID

Why do bulls charge?

t+
-N+Y
-A+
-e
+VY
CA+
-Fi

THEY SELDOM CARRY CASH

Why is Q impolite?

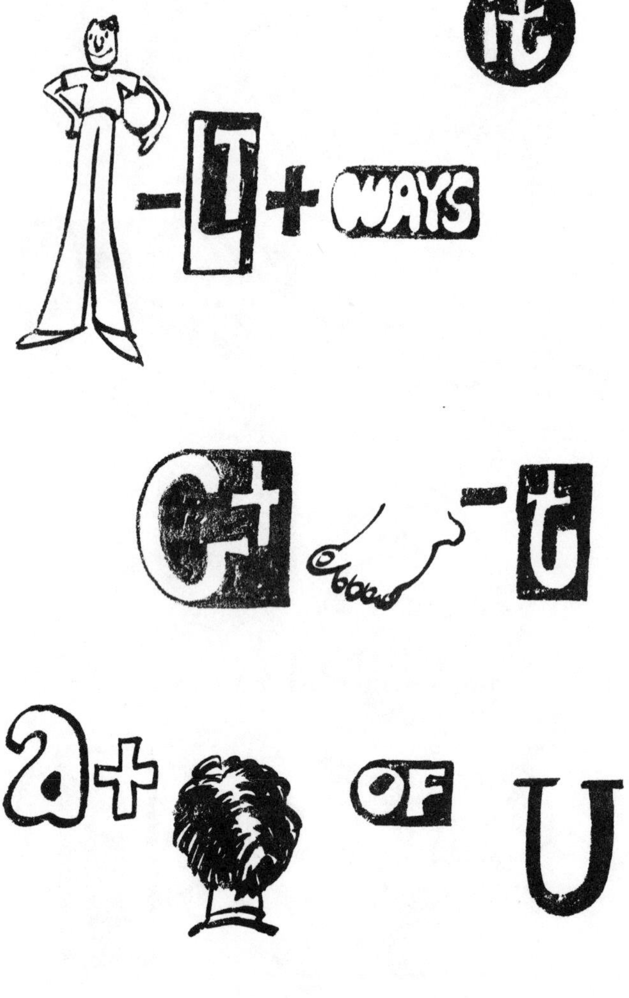
it
-LT+WAYS
G+ -t
a+ OF U

IT ALWAYS GOES AHEAD OF YOU (U)

How many legs does a race horse have?

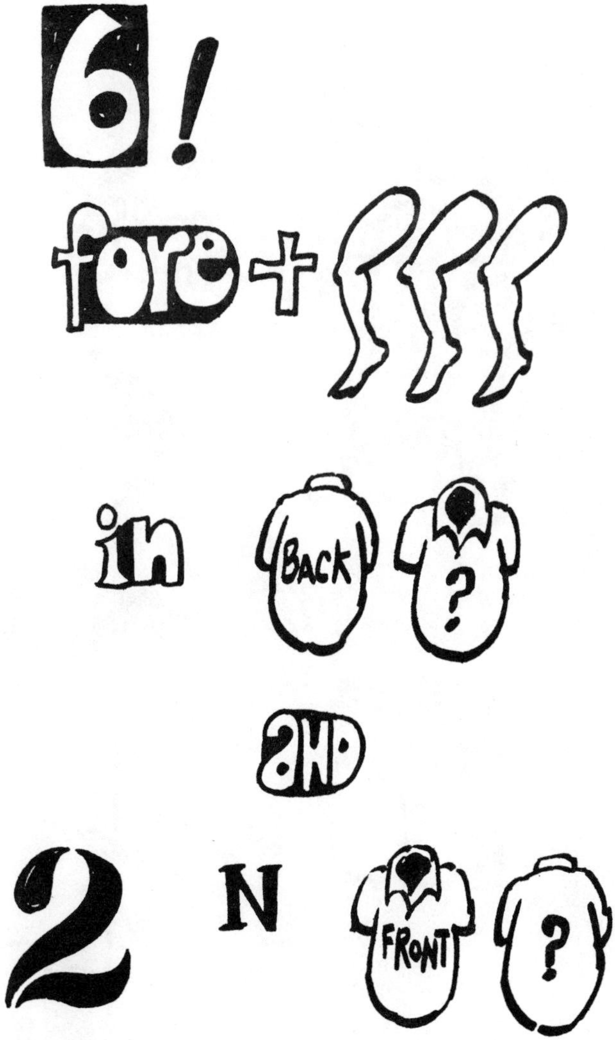

6!
fore +
in
BACK
?
2
N
FRONT
?

SIX! FOUR (FORE) LEGS IN FRONT AND TWO IN BACK

Why was the Joker wild?

HE
SOAP
-h+n't
PLAYING
-C
a
FUL
RAT
TAT.
d+
-P

HE WASN'T PLAYING WITH A FULL DECK

Why is a long road like a cat's tail?

It's
4-0
2
THE END

IT'S FUR (FAR) TO THE END

Index

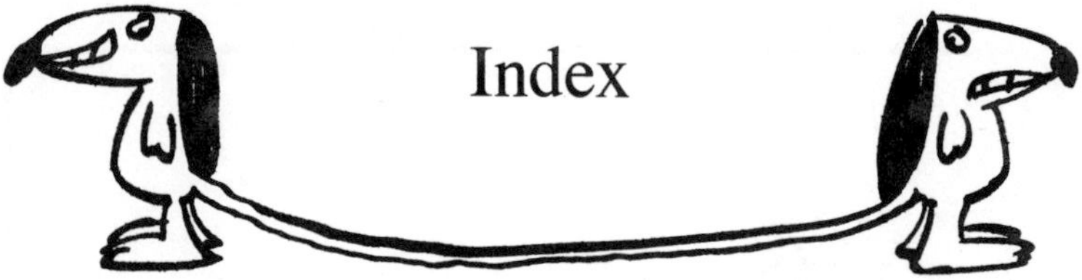

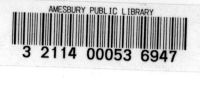